What Else Can

I Do With You?

A Lucky Duck Book

What Else Can I Do With You?

Helping Children Improve Classroom Behaviour

Second Edition

Fiona Wallace

P·C·P
Paul Chapman
Publishing

Paul Chapman Publishing
A SAGE Publications Company
1 Oliver's Yard
55 City Road
London EC1Y 1SP

SAGE Publications Inc.
2455 Teller Road
Thousand Oaks, California 91320

SAGE Publications India Pvt Ltd
B 1/I 1 Mohan Cooperative Industrial Area
Mathura Road, New Delhi 110 044

SAGE Publications Asia-Pacific Pte Ltd
33 Pekin Street #02-01
Far East Square
Singapore 048763

www.luckyduck.co.uk

Illustrator: Philippa Drakeford
Activity sheets designed by: Nick Shearn

British Library Cataloguing in Publication data

A catalogue record for this book is available from the British Library

ISBN 978 1 4129 2897 7

Library of Congress Control Number: 2006932493

Typeset by C&M Digitals (P) Ltd, Chennai, India
Printed in India by Replika Pvt, Ltd.
Printed on paper from sustainable resources

For Odile, with happy memories

Contents

Introduction

About this book

Nearly 20 years ago the Elton Report (Discipline in Schools. Report of the Committee of Inquiry, HMSO, 1989) described the problems that most concerned teachers at the time. These were not major behaviour difficulties such as violence and fighting but the persistent low-level disruption of behaviours such as talking out of turn, being out of seat, being disorganised, hindering others, lack of concentration and so on. These behaviours are still the focus of the DfES, which aims to 'help schools promote positive behaviour and tackle the issue of low-level disruption' (www.dfes.gov.uk/ibis/Department_policy/Behaviour.cfm). The issues tackled in *What Else Can I Do With You?* link well to the Change for Children agenda as well as the five outcomes in Every Child Matters, 2004.

These worksheets and activities are for those youngsters who are skilled at creating this low-level disruption. They have been devised to help staff working with primary and middle school age children in settings such as schools, learning support units, play schemes, before and after school clubs and mentoring groups. The worksheets provide a means of encouraging children to think about their behaviour and the effect of their actions in a constructively critical manner.

Some of the principles that guided the development of the materials are listed below:

- Staff must be able to deal effectively with a child in trouble without automatically attributing blame to the child or their actions.

- Adults can help children improve their behaviour without resorting to punishment or strategies based on deprivation of pleasurable activities or learning experiences.

- Children should take responsibility for their own actions, both those that get them into trouble and those that they can take to change their behaviour for the better. The worksheets provide a set of activities that encourage children to think about themselves and their actions in a constructive and critical manner. They provide opportunities to learn new skills that are less likely to get them into trouble.

- No child should be written off as beyond help and neither is any child perfect. There is always the chance to develop or strengthen skills and relationships and improve behaviour.

- Resources for busy staff must be easy to use. These sheets only need copying, which can be done freely within the purchasing establishment. The CD version enables sheets to be tailored to particular situations and put on the purchasing establishment's computer network, thus enabling easy access to the materials by a wide range of staff. The blank borders allow new sheets to be quickly designed to complement the published pack.

Before you start

These worksheets can be used in any way that will help children facing difficulties in group or classroom-type settings. However, they are not a shortcut solution to troublesome behaviour, nor are they an alternative to considering the effect of the environment and practices or how the behaviour of an adult or peer can set off a problem. Staff should keep their minds open to the idea that their own behaviour may need to be changed. The principle of using the least intrusive intervention to improve a situation should be adhered to – use a nutcracker not a sledge-hammer!

Before using any of these sheets with an individual pupil a period of observation should take place to ensure you are quite certain of exactly where changes need to be made and what those changes need to be, what behaviours should be encouraged and those that need to be changed.

Observation will, for example, clarify if the 'problem child' does indeed shout out more often than others in his or her group or if they just shout more loudly and are therefore heard every time, the others being a little quieter but calling out just as often. An approach to reduce shouting out might, therefore, best be targeted at the whole group rather than the loudest individual.

Observation would also indicate why a child is out of seat. This could be for a variety of reasons: because they are unable to do the activity and are asking for help from others; because they do not have all the equipment they need; because they are unable to maintain their attention; or because they have a low opinion of their skills and need frequent adult encouragement. Each of these reasons might require a different type of intervention, for example making equipment more accessible, building self-esteem, encouraging self-organisation or tackling a learning gap.

It is difficult to find time to step back and carefully observe and record what is going on in the setting but with planning and support from others this should be possible. A few 10-minute sessions at different times of the day, during different sessions or when the focus child is with different groups of children, will be time well spent; careful observation will mean the real difficulty can be addressed.

After gathering information through observation, you might use the following questions to guide your planning:

1.   What alerted you to the difficulty in the first place?
2.   What did you learn from careful observation?
3.   What is the behaviour you would like to change first?
4.   What has the child got to say about this behaviour?
5.   What plan have you and the child agreed on?
6.   When are you going to check on progress?
7.   How will you both know when you have successfully changed the behaviour?
8.   How will you celebrate and pass on the good news?

The tasks should be enjoyable. The activities will be less effective if thrust in front of the child in an attempt to keep them quiet. It will it not help to give the sheets as a punishment for the unwanted behaviour the sheet is intending to change. Threats such as 'If you don't remember to put your things away I'll make you stay in at break and do a sheet' will not put the child in the right frame of mind to learn from the message of the worksheet. All completed worksheets should be valued by the adult helper and the message of the task discussed with the child before and after doing the sheet. An easy way of doing this is to ask the child to show the completed sheet to another adult and explain what they have done and learned.

Many of the children who use these worksheets in school will be supported by a Pastoral Support Programme (PSP) or an Individual Education or Behaviour Plan (IE/BP) within the framework of the SEN Code of Practice. Careful record keeping will be needed. A suggested record sheet is included on the page following page xiii. Alternatively a note of any discussion with the child could be made on the back of a copy of the sheet, along with notes of your own thoughts and observations. Keeping a copy of the completed sheet will be helpful and it is good practice to ask the child's permission to do this. It is important to respect information the child has given as this may be confidential or could be misinterpreted if it gets out to a wider audience, for example, who the child dislikes or who gets him or her into trouble.

How To Use the CD-ROM

The CD-ROM contains a PDF file, labelled 'Worksheets.pdf'. You will need Acrobat Reader version 3 or higher to view and print these resources.

The documents are set up to print to A4 but you can enlarge them to A3 by increasing the output percentage at the point of printing using the page set-up settings for your printer.

Author's note
Insolence can be found three times in the word search on Worksheet 19.
The missing word for Worksheet 56 is 'share'.

Getting going

To complete any of the sheets the youngster will need a pencil and coloured pens or crayons. For some sheets scissors and a glue-stick will need to be available. Each activity should take the child around 10–15 minutes. The faster child should be encouraged to colour the borders to enhance the presentation of the finished worksheet. This activity will also keep them occupied for a little while allowing you to spend time with others and increasing the child's concentration span.

There are three types of worksheets in this book:

Problem specific worksheets

These sheets have been designed to cover those annoying, everyday problems that are so familiar to staff working with groups of children and are so disruptive to children's learning in the classroom. There is no right or wrong way for the pupil to complete the sheets. It is important to talk through with each child why you have given them a sheet to do, how you hope their behaviour will change and what they can do to make those changes. You must make this really clear! A child struggling to behave appropriately needs just as much structured help as one struggling to learn to read or spell new words. You can learn about the child and get new ideas for ways to help from the way they complete the worksheets; do not push a child into completing the worksheet the way you think it should be done!

The child who completed the sheet below (based on Worksheet 28, 'Politeness') was struggling with inter-personal relationships at an after-school club. The sheet was completed twice over a period of a few days, first relating to a Year 6 teacher and then

for the person in charge of the after-school club when it was linked to a discussion about being polite to all adults. The child was helped to realise that other adults as well as teachers had a right to politeness.

On some sheets the instruction *Write* has been given. If this makes it harder for a child to concentrate on the message of the task then simplify the task by writing the child's dictated words yourself or asking them to draw instead. These worksheets are not an exercise in writing or spelling; they are to help the child learn more appropriate behaviour and other learning may need to take a back seat until the behaviour skills are mastered.

Remember there will still be instances where a more detailed approach is appropriate – using these sheets first will help in making the decision to move to a greater level of support.

Open-ended sheets

It is not intended that every problem behaviour encountered in the classroom will be covered. Several open-ended sheets are included which can be used for a whole range of difficulties and allow children to reflect on a particular issue or situation that has arisen. In particular, pupils can think about their part in causing the problem and what they might do to put it right or prevent the situation from arising again.

Target sheets

The sheets in this section are in pairs, each designed to support children who need help to complete a number of tasks over part of a day, or longer. They can be used with the same child on several occasions. It is easy to change the level of difficulty of the task, either by increasing or reducing the number of tasks to be completed for each target sheet (more or less spots to be stuck on the ladybird) or by increasing or reducing the complexity of the tasks for each (longer or shorter activities on each playing card). Compare the three sets of targets on the next page.

Care needs to be taken to ensure the number and difficulty level of the tasks is realistic and achievable for the child. Nothing breeds success like success!

Blank borders

These blank borders enable new sheets to be designed for specific situations or with particular individuals in mind. The CD version of the book makes this even easier. Personalising the child's task will encourage them to do their best and will make it more memorable. You may wish to combine elements of two of the existing sheets or design a new one altogether. You are free to alter these sheets so they work as well as possible for the youngsters you are trying to help. Any new sheets you design should be kept with your master copies so that you or others can use them again, or perhaps even modify them in future to make yet more new sheets. Before you know it you will have a second book of sheets targeted at difficulties specific to your setting or pupils!

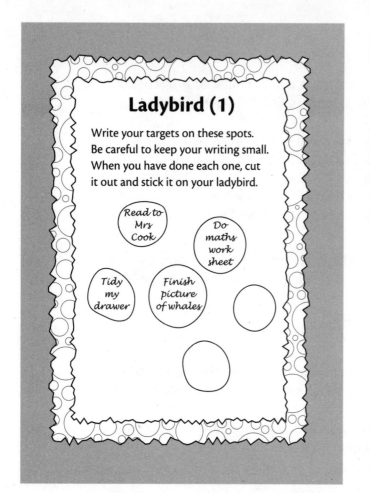

Ladybird (1)

Write your targets on these spots. Be careful to keep your writing small. When you have done each one, cut it out and stick it on your ladybird.

Read to Mrs Cook

Do maths work sheet

Tidy my drawer

Finish picture of whales

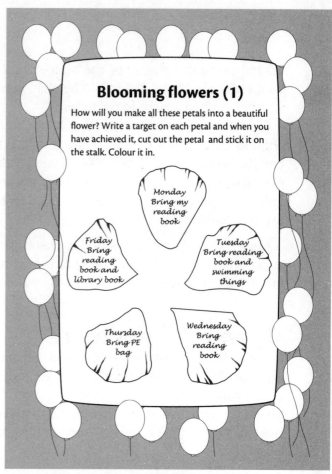

Blooming flowers (1)

How will you make all these petals into a beautiful flower? Write a target on each petal and when you have achieved it, cut out the petal and stick it on the stalk. Colour it in.

Monday Bring my reading book

Friday Bring reading book and library book

Tuesday Bring reading book and swimming things

Thursday Bring PE bag

Wednesday Bring reading book

Winning hand (1)

What do you need to do to get a winning hand? Write a target on each card. When you have achieved these targets cut them out and stick them on the hand to show your 'winning hand'.

A ♣ *Complete my work without disturbing others up to play time* ♣ A

A ♦ *Complete my work without disturbing others from play to lunch time* ♦ A

A ♠ *Complete my work without disturbing others from lunch to play time* ♠ A

A ♥ *Complete my work without disturbing others from play to home time* ♥ A

Further reading and resources

There are, of course, numerous resources both printed and online addressing problem behaviour in the classroom and other settings. A selection of those with very practical advice and suggestions is given below. Unless otherwise mentioned the publications are available in the Incentive Plus catalogue.

The *Incentive Plus* catalogue is full of posters, games books and other resources (including Lucky Duck Books) in the area of behaviour and emotional literacy.

Incentive Plus   Tel (UK) 01908 526120
6 Fernfield Farm   www.incentiveplus.co.uk
Little Horwood
Milton Keynes
MK17 0PR

Many of the photocopiable activities in *Not You Again!* by Fiona Wallace and Diane Caesar will also help the child struggling with appropriate 'classroom' behaviour. A third book, *Just Stop... and Think!*, by Fiona Wallace, provides a range of activities, also photocopiable, aimed at helping children plan improvements in their behaviour in a step by step manner. Both are Lucky Duck books published by Paul Chapman Publishing.

Managing Successful Inclusion – *The Pastoral Support Programme in Practice* (E. Smith and W.D. MacPherson, 2000), guides you through the PSP process and gives all the necessary forms. It is available from:

AMS Educational   Tel (UK) 0113 258 0309
Woodside Trading Estate   www.senter.co.uk
Low Lane
Horsforth
Leeds   LS18 5NY

In *Celebrations*, a book of photocopiable certificates from George Robinson and Barbara Maines of Lucky Duck, there are enough certificates for every school day of the year, even a leap year! They cover a wide range of behaviours, including many that are not traditionally rewarded. Enjoy browsing the website at www.luckyduck. co.uk.

Classroom Survival Skills and *Student Survival Skills Audit* are two of several highly practical resources written by Rob Long. *Classroom Survival Skills* contains a number of photocopiable booklets for use with secondary pupils who want to improve self-control, organisational skills and so on. *Student Survival Skills* allows a primary or secondary pupil working with an adult to produce a visual profile of their strengths and weaknesses in areas that affect school success, such as learning skills and friendships.

For those of you wanting ideas for staff development activities in the area of behaviour management, get hold of a copy of *100 Activities for Behaviour Management Training Days* by Dave Vizard, the founder of Behaviour Solutions. These activities have been tried and tested in schools across the country and cover issues such as understanding the importance of body language and developing a consistent approach. There is a long list of useful links on Dave's website at www.behaviourmatters.com from which you can also order his books.

'Framework for Intervention' – This project, initiated in Birmingham, helps teachers tackle concerns about students' behaviour in schools and nurseries, using school improvement, staff empowerment and environmental change. It works for all ages and in all settings, promoting 'Learning behaviour together': www.frameworkforintervention.com. Project materials are available through the website or from Incentive Plus.

For those of you who never have time to read anything other than the back of a cereal packet, there is a series of DVDs presented by Bill Rogers covering *'Prevention', 'Positive Correction', 'Consequences'* and *'Repair and Rebuild'*. The DVDs are easy to watch and each is about 40 minutes long, presented in a different style. You could dip in and out of them, but time taken to view 'Positive Correction' would be time well spent. Watching as a staff group would lead to a valuable discussion about managing behaviour in your setting.

Session record sheet

Pupil .... Date of session ....

☐ Not You Again!

☐ What Else Can I Do With You?   Worksheet number

☐ Just Stop ... and Think!

Worksheet title.......................................Staff initials...

Key points from this session

Actions for staff (What? Who? When?)

Issues for exploration at a future session

Review of progress made in this area   Date ....

Trouble bubbles

Write your troubles in the bubbles.
Put the biggest trouble in the biggest bubble.

Now close your eyes and imagine the bubbles floating away
with your troubles inside.

Watch them burst and disappear!

Your name _____   Helper's name _____

Angry thoughts

Angry thoughts are not helpful. They can make you do things that get you into trouble. They can make you feel sad and miserable.

Write down some of your angry thoughts.

Next time you think these thoughts try to keep calm by counting to 10 slowly. If you still feel a bit angry count back from 10 to 0 while you stretch out your fingers.

Write down one time when you will try this.

Your name _____

Helper's name _____

Look at you

Draw how you look when you are really angry. Think carefully about how to do your face and your hands.

Now draw or write 4 things that you can do to make you feel calmer.

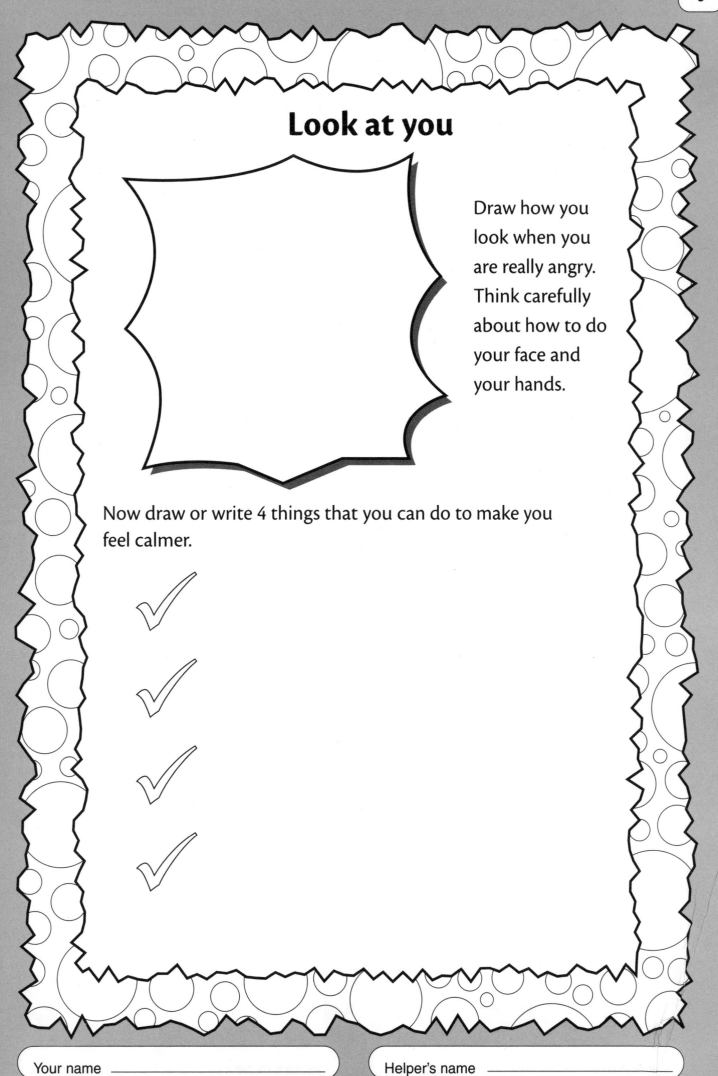

Your name _____

Helper's name _____

Losing your temper

What makes you lose your temper?

-
-
-
-
-

Next time you think you are going to lose your temper try this:

1. Take a deep breath

2. Count to 10 slowly

3. Let your breath out slowly

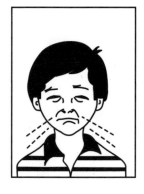  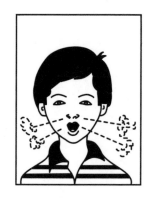

Do this exercise 5 more times. How do you feel now?

Your name _____   Helper's name _____

TV characters

Think of all the good helpful characters you see on TV.
Draw your favourite.

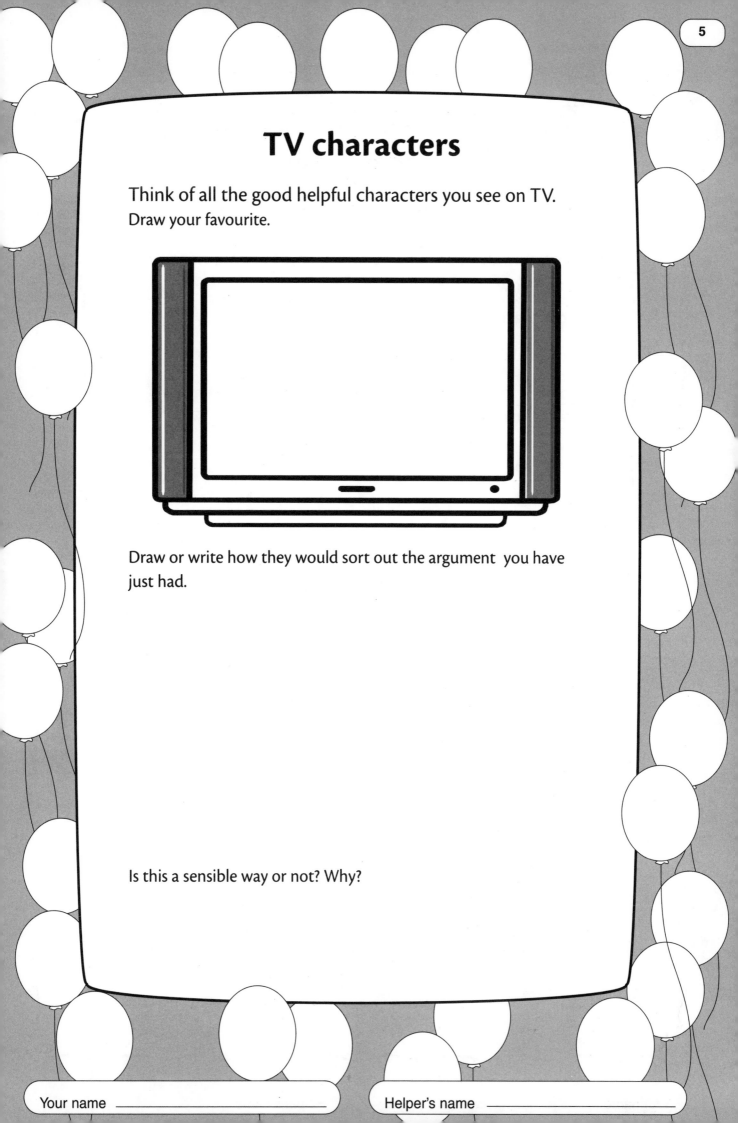

Draw or write how they would sort out the argument you have
just had.

Is this a sensible way or not? Why?

Your name _____   Helper's name _____

Patience! Patience!

No pushing, no shoving ... Just be patient!

While you wait you could do one of these in your head. Have a practice now.

Count backwards from 100 in 3s.

Say the alphabet backwards.

Think of something in school for every letter of the alphabet. Have a go now.

A	N
B	O
C	P
D	Q
E	R
F	S
G	T
H	U
I	V
J	W
K	X
L	Y
M	Z

What will you do next time you have to wait?

Your name _____

Helper's name _____

Line up please!

We line up so that we can move around the building without making a crowd in the corridor. Why else do we line up? Tick the right ones.

So we can move along more quickly ☐ So the teachers can carry everything ☐

So other people can pass easily ☐ So we don't talk and make too much noise ☐

So no one sees us ☐ So the classroom is empty ☐

To keep stairs and doorways safe ☐ To make it easy to count the children ☐

Draw yourself in the line at the door or in the playground.

Put up your hand

Draw around your hand. On each finger write one reason why it is better to put up your hand than to call out.

If you get stuck you can put up your hand and ask for help. This will not disturb the other children and an adult will come to you when they can.

Your name _____   Helper's name _____

Who helps and who makes it hard?

Write the names of 4 children in your class along the top row. Read the list of behaviours down the side. Put a tick or a cross to show whether it is true or not for that child.

Names				
talks too much in class				
lets me finish my work				
messes with other kids				
calls out in class				
tries hard with work				

Who helps you get on with your work?

Your name _____

Helper's name _____

Rest your legs ...
Put up your hand

Each time you remember to put up your hand you can colour in one section of the hand picture. When the hand is all coloured put up your hand and show it to your teacher.

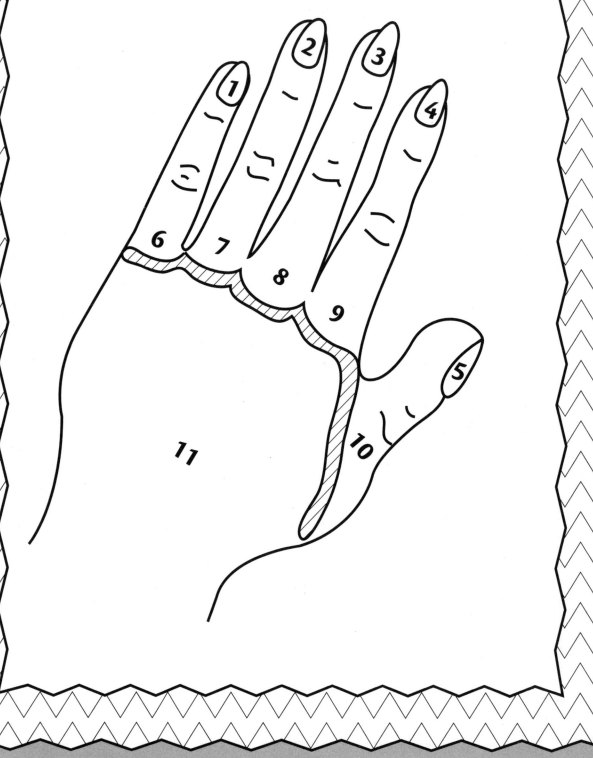

Shopping List

If you could go to the supermarket and buy good behaviour for your group what would you want to buy? Try to finish the list.

A packet of cheerfulness

2 boxes of ...

4 bags of ...

2 ...   of smiles

A tin of ...

1 large ...

2 ...   of tidiness

A bottle of ...

These are some words which might help to finish the list:

thinkers	hard work	helpfulness
kindness	quietness	carefulness

Tick the things you need most. How could you get them?

Your name _____   Helper's name _____

Feelings

Make a blue cross on the lines to show how you feel when you are in trouble.

sad _____ happy

clever _____ silly

embarrassed _____ proud

pleased _____ cross

big _____ small

confident _____ scared

Now put a red tick on each line to show how you would like to feel.

Think of two ways that you could change what you do to feel nearer to the ticks than the crosses.

Your name _____   Helper's name _____

Throwing

I should not throw things in the classroom because:

Draw

I might hurt someone.

Draw

I might break something.

Other people matter

Think about how another child feels if you spoil their work.
Draw the faces to show the feelings.

sad

angry

How could you make these children feel happy again?

Your name _____ Helper's name _____

Look and listen

This is what your teacher wants to see when she is talking to you all. All the children are listening to the teacher.

Draw the faces in. Don't forget the ears for listening.

What helps you to listen well?

Your name _____   Helper's name _____

Listening is very important

Write down a list of all the sounds that you can hear now and sort them into the ones which are in the room and the ones which come from outside.

In the room	Outside

Draw a small picture of you listening really carefully to someone talking.

The Green Cross Code

Stop   when your teacher or helper asks

Look   at them when they are speaking to you

Listen   carefully to what is said

Draw some road signs to help you remember these three steps.

Your name _____

Helper's name _____

18

Make a poster to remind all the children to remember the rule:

We work without disturbing others

Your name _____

Helper's name _____

Insolence

Do you know what insolence means? Ask someone or look it up in the dictionary. Tick the right meaning.

☐ not thinking enough   ☐ being silly

☐ making rude noises   ☐ teasing

☐ being cheeky and disrespectful   ☐ being careless

How many times can you find the word insolence in the word search?

f	i	e	c	n	e	l	o	s	n	i
y	n	e	r	a	s	c	f	r	h	e
k	s	s	h	c	v	b	n	m	c	t
e	o	c	j	b	s	r	o	n	j	y
c	l	f	k	h	t	j	e	l	k	u
i	e	v	n	m	f	l	s	e	o	n
n	n	g	l	t	o	h	r	t	u	j
t	c	w	o	s	d	i	n	s	p	i
m	e	s	n	r	r	y	s	o	l	k
i	i	i	p	g	r	d	s	w	e	q

I found *insolence* _____ times in this word search.

Your name _____   Helper's name _____

Word Search

Make a word search. Put in all these things that you can do in the classroom without being told off.

think   work   draw   write

learn   listen   smile   read

help   paint   discuss

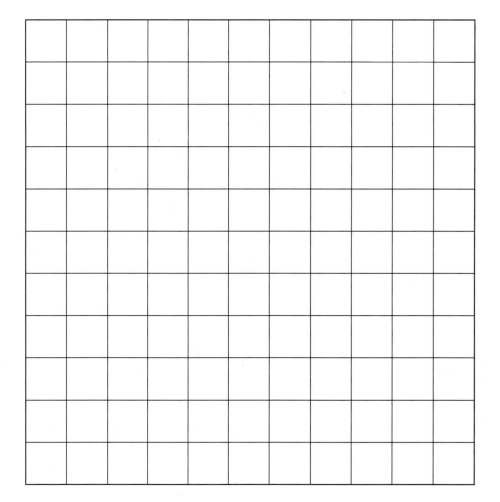

Give your word search to a friend to do.

Make a poster to remind all the children to remember the rule:

Keep everything in its proper place

Your name _____   Helper's name _____

Make a poster to remind all the children to remember the rule:

Only speak to each other in a kind and friendly way

Your name _____

Helper's name _____

No running

I should not run around the room because:

Draw

I might disturb others.

Draw

I might knock somebody's work.

Your name _____   Helper's name _____

No shouting out

I should not shout out because:

Draw

I might disturb others.

Draw

Everyone should have a chance to talk.

Your name _____   Helper's name _____

Red   Amber   Green

Colour the traffic lights the correct colours
Write down when you should . . .

Not talk at all

•

•

•

Talk quietly to your neighbours

•

•

•

Talk to anyone in the room

•

•

•

Your name _____   Helper's name _____

Name calling

1. Everyone feels sad when they are called an unkind name.
   Do you ever call anyone an unkind name?

   Yes ☐   No ☐

2. Do you feel good if you upset someone?

   Yes ☐   No ☐

3. Sort the names into two sets and write them in the boxes below.

   thicko   mate   cow   dear   star

   love   idiot   creep   dummy

   weedy   pet   friend   fatty   cool

   wicked   spotty   brainy   gorgeous

Kind	**Unkind**

It's how you say it ...

The way we say things is important. There are unkind ways to say things and more helpful words. Match the unkind words to the more helpful way of saying them.

Get out of my way, you fathead

Oi! Gimme the scissors. You've had them ages.

Clear off! We don't want you in our group.

Shut up talking – you're doing my head in!

Have you nearly finished with the scissors? Can I have them next, please?

I can't concentrate if you talk so much. Please be quieter, thanks.

Can I come past, please?

We don't need anyone else in our group. Maybe you can join next time.

Now think of your own pair:

Your name _____

Helper's name _____

Politeness

Always try to be polite.

Draw the person in charge in the frame.

What should this person say to you if you have been rude to a grown up?

1.

2.

3.

What will you do next time?

Your name _____

Helper's name _____

Think!

What would you do if ...

Someone knocked your books off the table?

Someone pushed past your chair and knocked your work?

Someone wouldn't share the crayons?

Someone took your rubber without asking?

Are your ideas good or are they going to cause trouble?
Put a tick by the ideas that are good.

Your name _____   Helper's name _____

Keep Safe

Which of these things have you got in your classroom?
Draw them.
Put a red circle around the ones which could be
dangerous and have to be used very carefully.

hole punch

scissors   pens

paint

guillotine

glue

craft knives

hammer

drawing pins

rulers   rubber

stapler

Your name _____   Helper's name _____

Maths bookmark

What do you need to remember most each time you settle down to work on your numeracy?

Make yourself a bookmark to keep in your maths book so that each time you open the book and look at it you will be reminded what you need to do.

1. Write or draw your message and colour your bookmark.

2. Cut it out.

3. Fold along the dotted line and glue it together to make it strong.

4. When it is dry keep it in your maths book.

5. Read it each time you open your book.

back   front

Maths

Your name _____

Helper's name _____

Literacy bookmark

What do you need to remember most each time you settle down to work on your literacy?

Make yourself a bookmark to keep in your literacy book so that each time you open the book and look at it you will be reminded what you need to do.

back   front

Literacy

1. Write or draw your message and colour your bookmark.

2. Cut it out.

3. Fold along the dotted line and glue it together to make it strong.

4. When it is dry keep it in your literacy book.

5. Read it each time you open your book.

Your name _____

Helper's name _____

School bag

What do you need to remember for each school day?
Draw the things you should put in a school bag. Choose
from the list:

pencils   comic   pens   crisps   ruler   scissors   rubber

crayons   felt pens   notebook

gloves   lunch money   sandwich box   PE kit

reading book   toys   drink

Write 2 ideas to help you remember to bring these things.

-
-

Your name _____   Helper's name _____

PE bag

What things do you need to remember for PE?
Draw them in a PE bag and label them. Choose from
the list below:

shorts	felt pens	comic	T-shirt	pens
hat	trainers	sweets		trousers
tracksuit	leotard	ruler	pumps	swimsuit
towel	reading book		socks	

Your name _____

Helper's name _____

Good news

Who should hear good news about how you are working? Draw your teacher talking to that person. Fill in the speech bubbles.

Your name _____

Helper's name _____

Medals

What have you done this week that you are really proud of?
Design a medal to celebrate your success.

My medal is for ....

Your name _____   Helper's name _____

Send a text

Do u no how 2 txt?

Write 2 messages on the phone screens to tell people what things you are trying to improve on.

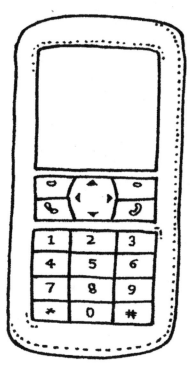

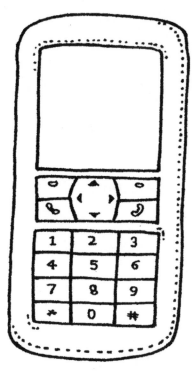

Send this text to ...

Send this text to ...

How could these people help you?

Your name _____

Helper's name _____

Hip... hip... hooray!

Why do you deserve three cheers?

Write down three reasons why the staff can be pleased with you.

Hip ...

Hip ...

Hooray

Now think of three reasons why your friends can be pleased with you.

Hip ...

Hip ...

Hooray

Picture him

Here is a boy with brown hair and a blue shirt sitting at his table. He is sad. Someone has spoilt his work.

Draw the picture.

What do you suggest to make him feel happier?

Your name _____   Helper's name _____

Picture her

Here is a girl with long hair and a green jumper sitting at her table. She is sad. Someone has spoilt her work.

Draw the picture.

What do you suggest to make her feel happier?

Helping others

These children need help.
How could you help them?

Draw the people and write what you would say.

> 'It is too noisy
> in here for me
> to do my work.'

> 'I can't find my
> reading book.'

Being helpful?

These children need help.
How could you help them?

Draw the people and write what you would say.

'I can't remember
what I should do.'

'No one will lend me
any felt pens to finish
my picture.'

Your name _____

Helper's name _____

Sit comfortably

Make a notice to remind all the children to sit safely on the chairs. Put in your notice 2 reasons why it is not good to swing back on the chairs.

Your name _____

Helper's name _____

'Wait your turn'

Imagine this is the title of a new book. The chapters could be called:

1.   Do not push.

2.   You cannot always be first.

3.   Be patient.

Design a cover for the book.

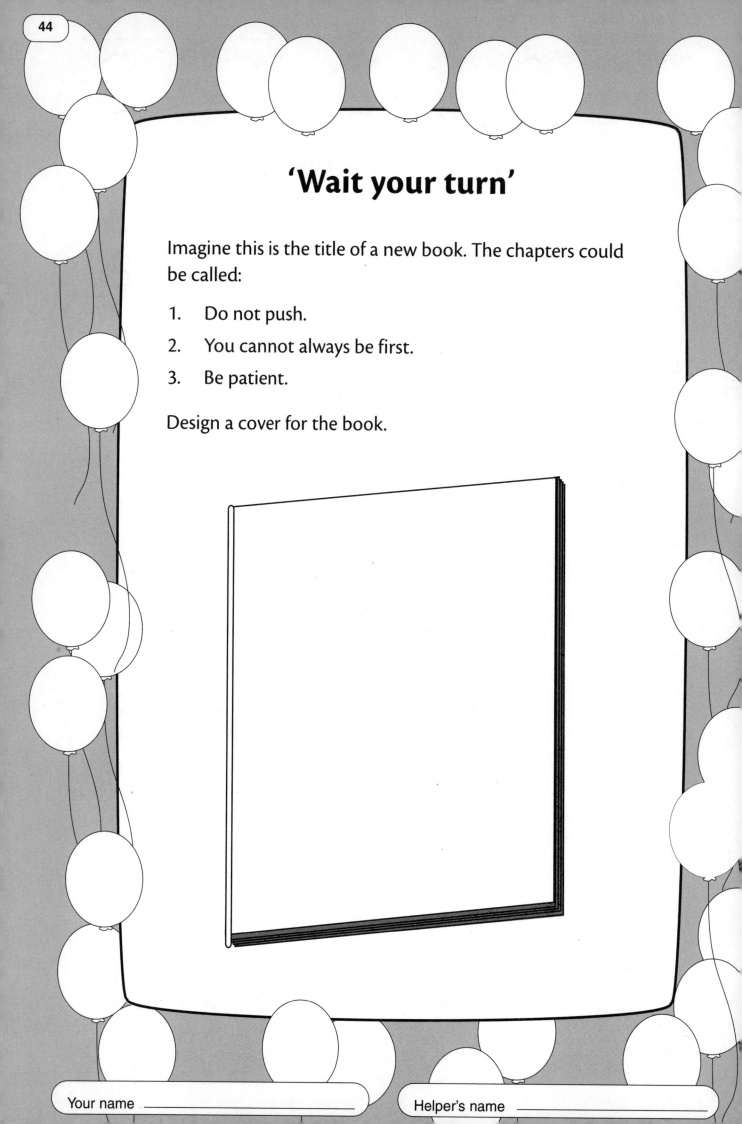

Your name _____   Helper's name _____

Classroom acrostic

Can you finish this acrostic to remind you how to behave in the classroom?

C alling out ...

L isten to ...

A lways ...

S peak quietly when ...

S it ...

R aise your hand to ...

O nly ...

O ther children ...

M ake sure ...

Your name _____

Helper's name _____

What do you do in the classroom?

Put a tick in the right column.

	never	sometimes	a lot
finish your work			
feel sad			
sit quietly			
work with other children			
sit by yourself			
work with friends			
feel worried			
stay by the teacher			
run about			
work alone			
have fun			
feel cross			
work with girls			
work with boys			
ask for help			
remember your pencil case			

What will you do to improve?

Your name _____

Helper's name _____

Stop! Think!

Why should you wait for your turn and not push in?
Draw some of your ideas.

Happy classrooms

If we all work together we can have a happy classroom. How can you help?

Write your ideas.

'I can ...
pick things up
off the floor'.

'I can ...

'I can ...

'I can ...

Draw the children helping.

Your name _____

Helper's name _____

Safe chairs

Do not swing on your chair!

Draw

You might fall off.

Draw

The chair might break.

Your name _____

Helper's name _____

Sit safely

Do not swing on your chair!

Draw

Somebody might trip over you.

Draw

You might block the way.

Your name _____

Helper's name _____

Too much talk

Sometimes we all talk too much. Grown-ups might use a funny saying to keep everyone quiet ...

Button your lip!

Put a sock in it!

Why do we need to talk less?

1.

2.

3.

Counting the minutes

Can you work for minutes without stopping?

Fill in the time you start on the top clock.
Work hard for as long as you can.
Fill in the time you finish on the bottom clock.

Start

Finish

How many minutes did you work without stopping?

Did you finish the task? Circle your answer:

Yes   No   Nearly

Your name _____   Helper's name _____

Inside – Outside

Which things usually happen inside and which happen outside? Sort the list into the right sets. Some things can be in both. Can you put any more things in the sets?

classroom

playground

singing

shouting

sharpening pencils

telling jokes

hopping

working

running

reading

thinking

drawing

sitting

whistling

football

humming

Your name _____

Helper's name _____

Job done!

These children have finished their work.
Draw what they will choose to do next.

 Jay has
finished
his work.

 Anita has
finished
her work.

What would you
choose to do when
you have finished
all your work?

Your name _____

Helper's name _____

Finish it all!

Can you carefully colour all of this picture and the border without getting up from your seat or disturbing anybody?

If you get stuck put your hand up and ask for help.

Your name _____   Helper's name _____

Find the missing word

One of these words is **<u>not</u>** in this word search. Which is it?

listen   share   try

concentrate   help   tidy

think   support   careful

work   cooperate   quiet

w	o	r	k	a	c	s	d	r	j	t	m
f	a	t	b	p	h	o	x	p	g	h	e
u	h	x	q	b	t	s	l	z	u	i	p
e	l	b	u	s	y	e	n	h	a	n	h
t	i	n	i	v	h	n	w	o	r	k	l
a	s	v	e	r	t	r	g	h	f	m	m
r	t	q	t	t	s	u	p	p	o	r	t
t	e	o	c	e	c	l	r	d	k	t	e
n	n	p	y	o	u	g	x	y	d	i	t
e	j	d	o	f	k	r	h	b	i	f	v
c	e	w	e	w	a	z	d	j	u	l	k
n	q	r	f	z	g	s	b	d	j	q	s
o	a	n	c	o	o	p	e	r	a	t	e
c	g	m	w	l	x	y	r	t	k	y	c

On the back draw yourself doing what the missing word says.

Can you do this?

What have all these children been doing to help them get on with their work? Follow the lines and write the letters to find out.

Dan

Robina

Luke

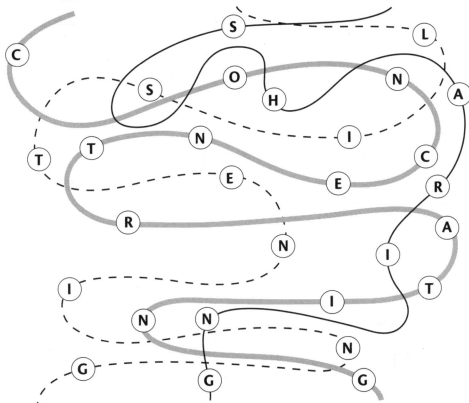

Robina is

_ _ _ _ _ _ _ _

Luke is

_ _ _ _ _ _ _ _

Dan is

_ _ _ _ _ _ _ _

How could you be better at these things?

Your name _____   Helper's name _____

Swimming

Circle all the things you should remember to bring for swimming.

towel   costume

money   hat   trunks

shampoo   bag   comb

brush   drink   food

Circle which day you will need these things.

Monday

Tuesday

Wednesday

Thursday

Friday

Colour the border then take this notice home and put it up where you can see it so that it will remind you to bring your swimming things on the right day.

Your name _____   Helper's name _____

PE and Games

Circle all the things you should remember to bring for PE and games lessons.

towel   pumps

shorts   trainers   leotard

shampoo   bag   comb

brush   T-shirt   socks

football boots   track suit

Circle which day you will need these things.

Monday

Tuesday

Wednesday

Thursday

Friday

Colour the border then take this notice home and put it up where you can see it so that it will remind you to bring your PE and games kit on the right day.

Your name _____   Helper's name _____

Lessons

Draw all the things you need for this lesson.

pens	rubber	paper
scissors	writing book	glue
workbook	sharpener	pencil

Is there anything else you need?

Now collect your things and get started!

Get ready

Make a list of all the things you will need for this lesson.
There are some words to remind you at the bottom
of the page.

1.

2.

3.

4.

5.

6.

7.

8.

ruler   felt pens   rough book   rubber

maths book   sharpener   crayons   reading book   worksheet

pen   paper   scissors   pencil   writing book   glue

Now get started!

Your name _____   Helper's name _____

Help yourself

Try to help yourself before asking your teacher.

Would any of these ideas help?

Ask your neighbour
Think carefully
Read the worksheet again
Look what others are doing

Draw yourself working hard without any help from the teacher.

Your name _____

Helper's name _____

Sssshhhh!!!

We work quietly in class:

    so other children can work
    so everyone can hear the teacher
    so people can think properly
    so you can get on with your work

Draw yourself working quietly without disturbing anybody.

Your name _____

Helper's name _____

When is it ...

Good to talk?

Sometimes it is best to work quietly and sometimes it is OK to talk to somebody while you work.

Draw one picture for a time when you work quietly and one for a time when you can talk.

Working quietly

OK to talk quietly

Your name _____   Helper's name _____

I feel ...

If someone spoilt your work how would you feel?
Draw or write your answer.

Make a note of 3 things that would make you feel better.

•

•

•

Your name _____

Helper's name _____

How does he feel?

Somebody has scribbled on his work. Draw or write
how he feels.

Luke

Can you think of 3 ideas to help him feel better?

-
-
-

Your name _____   Helper's name _____

Happy endings

Draw the pictures.

1

Jo pushes past Sam

2

Sam falls over and cries

3

Jo laughs at Sam

Draw a new picture for number 3 to make the story have a happy ending.

Make a story-board

Something has happened to upset this boy. How could you help to cheer him up?

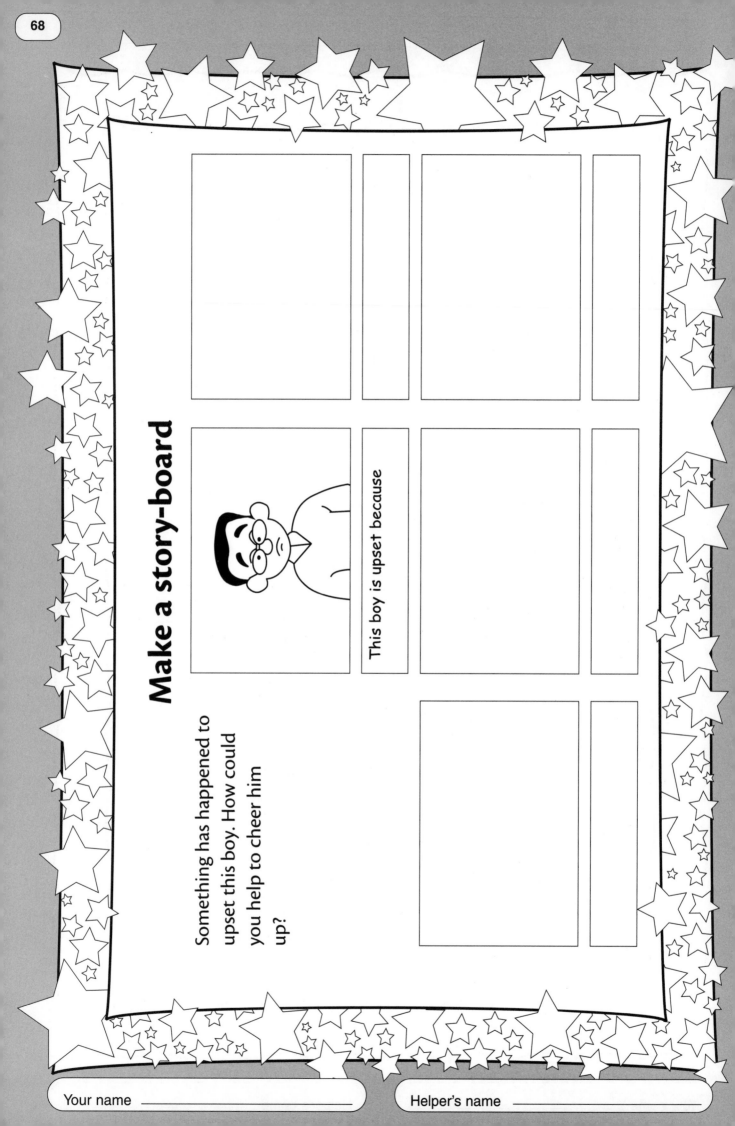

This boy is upset because

Puzzle it out

What went wrong today?	Who was upset?
Next time things will be better because I will ...	Why did this happen?

Your name _____

Helper's name _____

Mend your ways

How did it all go wrong today?

Why did this happen?

How can you mend your ways?

Your name _____   Helper's name _____

Turn over a new leaf

Why are you in trouble?

How did this happen?

What will you do next time?

Your name _____

Helper's name _____

Wipe the slate clean

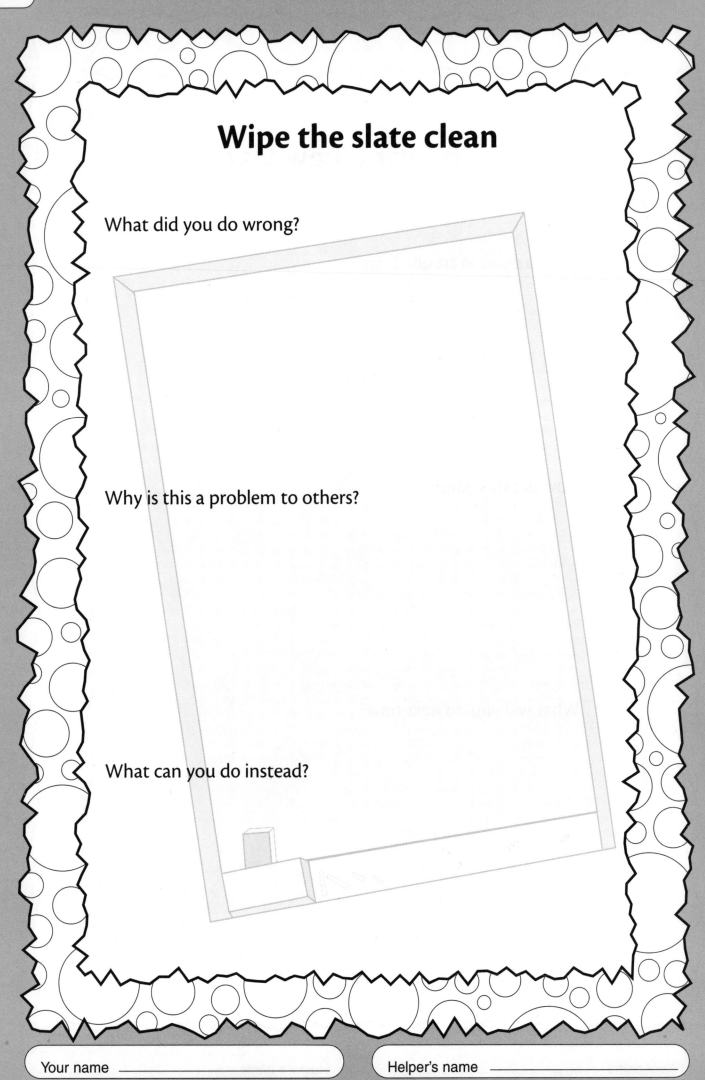

What did you do wrong?

Why is this a problem to others?

What can you do instead?

Your name _____   Helper's name _____

Yummy! (1)

Here are two layers of cake, some jam and some icing.
Write a good thing to do on each slice.

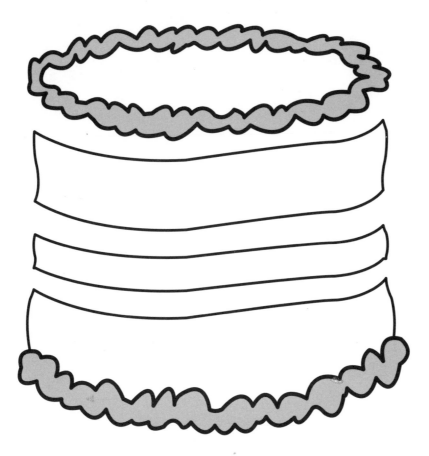

Write a really nice treat for yourself on this candle.

Now cut out the sections and stick them on the plate
when you have done each task.

Stick the candle on the top when you have had your treat!

Your name _____   Helper's name _____

Yummy! (2)

This delicious cake is made of good things I have done!
I had my treat on_____

Your name _____   Helper's name _____

You can be proud of yourself! (1)

On each section of the shield write something you are going to do that you are proud of. Decorate each piece and when you have done the tasks stick the shield together and claim your reward.

Your name _____   Helper's name _____

You can be proud of yourself! (2)

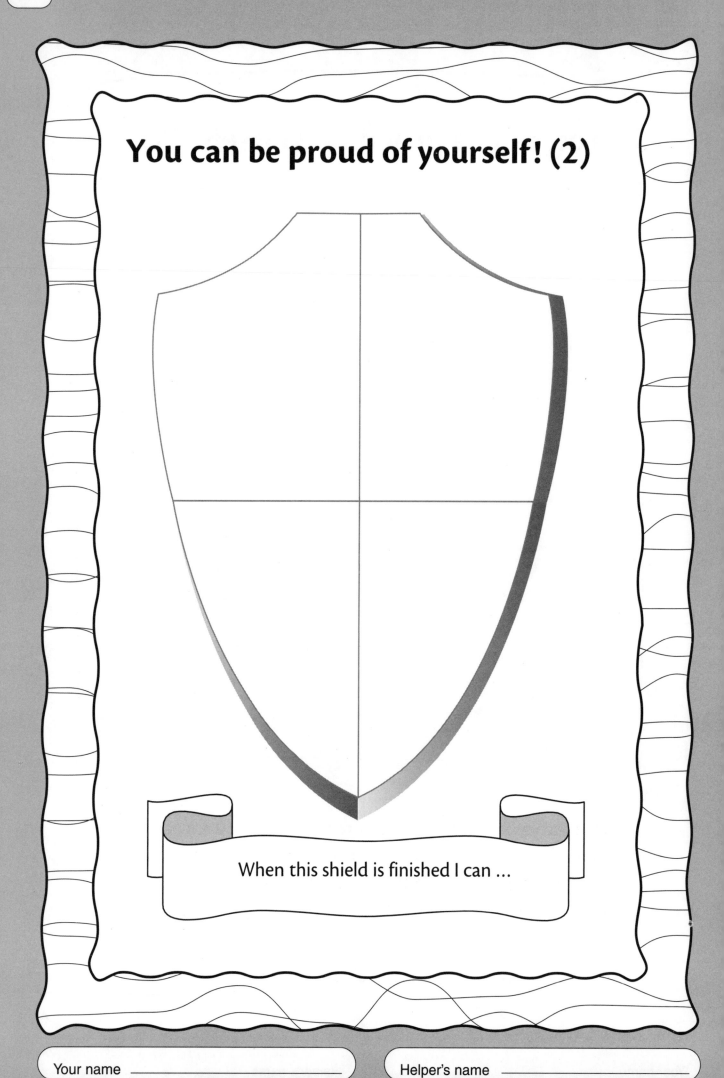

When this shield is finished I can …

Your name _____

Helper's name _____

Basketball (1)

These balls can go into the basket when you reach your target. Write one thing you need to do on each ball. When you have done each one, cut out the ball and stick it in the basket.

Your name _____   Helper's name _____

Basketball (2)

I am going to get all my shots in the basket by _____.

When I have scored ⬚ I can ...

Football (1)

What are your goals? Write them on these footballs.
When you've done one, cut out the ball and stick it in
the goal.

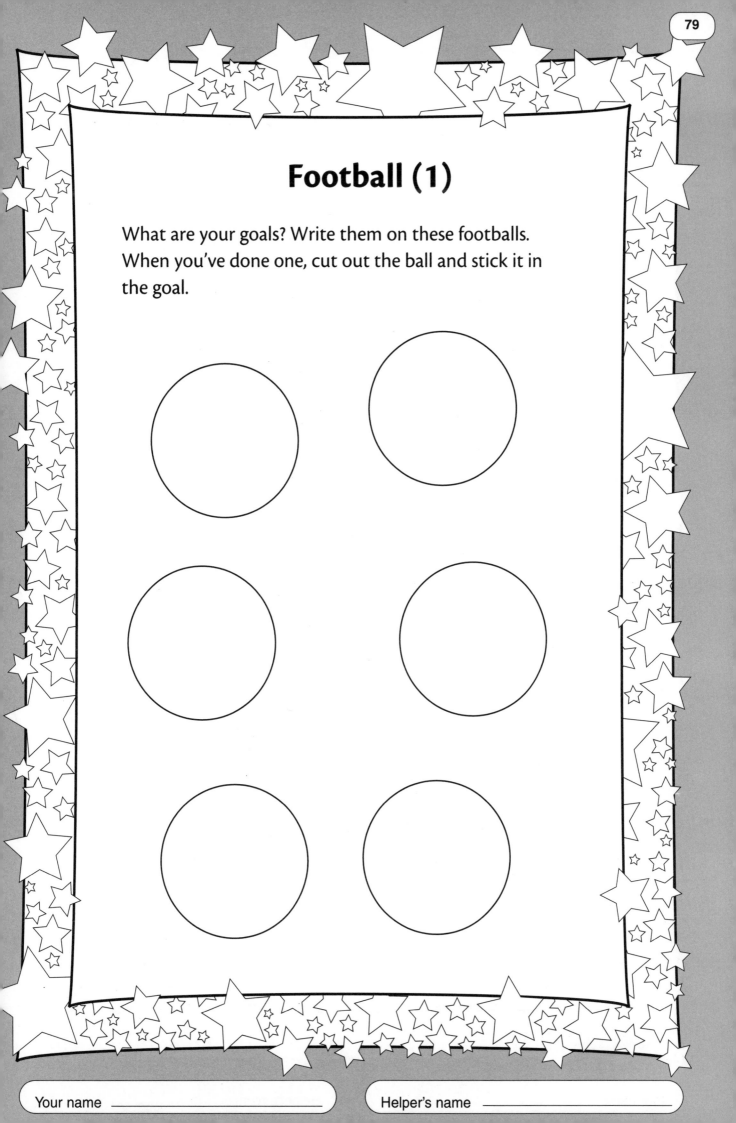

Your name _____   Helper's name _____

Football (2)

I will score ☐ goals by _____

When I have done them all I can …

Winning hand (1)

What do you need to do to get a winning hand? Write a target on each card. When you have achieved these targets cut them out and stick them on the hand to show your 'winning hand'.

A ♣	A ♦
A ♠	A ♥

Your name _____

Helper's name _____

Winning hand (2)

Here are my 4 aces

When I have achieved these targets I can choose to ...

Your name _____   Helper's name _____

Ladybird (1)

Write your targets on these spots. Be careful to keep your writing small. When you have done each one, cut it out and stick it on your ladybird.

Your name _____

Helper's name _____

Ladybird (2)

When you have stuck on all the spots draw two antennae on your ladybird and then you can …

Your name _____   Helper's name _____

Blooming flowers (1)

How will you make all these petals into a beautiful flower?
Write a target on each petal and when you have achieved it,
cut out the petal and stick it on the stalk. Colour it in.

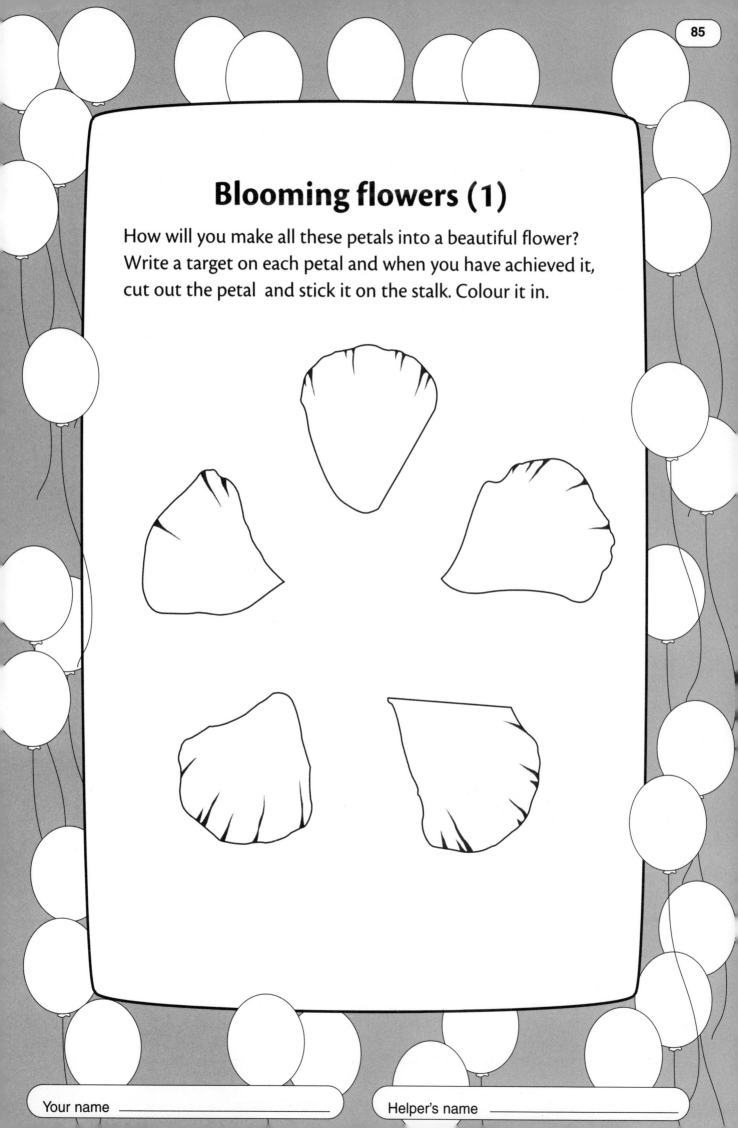

Your name _____

Helper's name _____

Blooming Flowers (2)

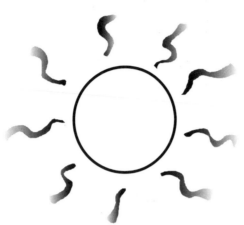

This flower is going to
open all its petals by

When the petals have all opened I can do what it says on the sun.

Your name _____   Helper's name _____

Bookshelf (1)

Fill in the title of each book with one thing that you should do. When you achieve each target cut out the book and stick it on the bookshelf.

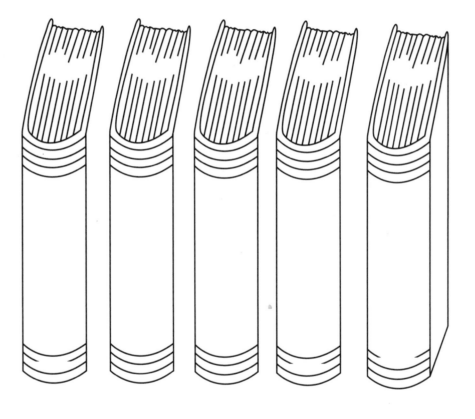

Bookshelf (2)

When there are ⬚ books on the shelf I can …

House (1)

This house has four windows. Fill in a target on each one.
You will have to keep your writing small! When you have
achieved the target, cut out the window and stick it
on to the house.

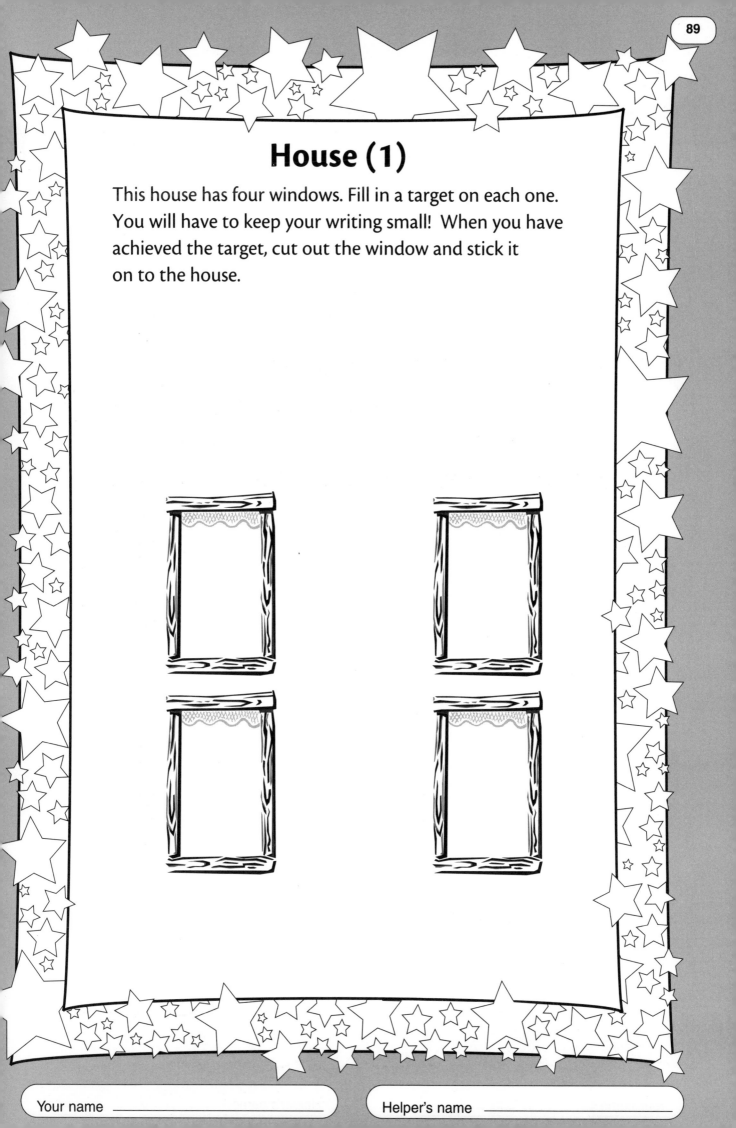

Your name _____

Helper's name _____

House (2)

When you have put all the windows on to the house you can do what is written on the door.

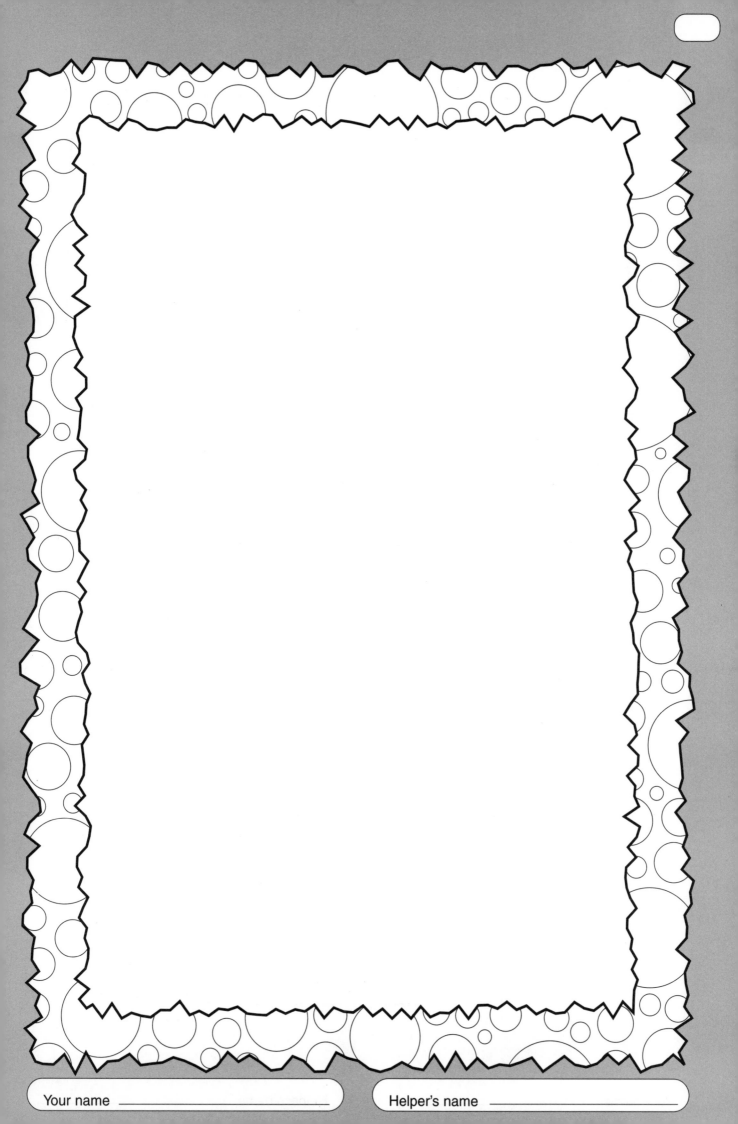

Your name _____   Helper's name _____

Your name _____   Helper's name _____

Your name _____

Helper's name _____

Your name _____   Helper's name _____

Your name _____

Helper's name _____

Your name _____

Helper's name _____